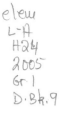

elew
L-A
H24
2005
Gr.1
D.Bk.9

DECODABLE BOOK 9

Orlando   Boston   Dallas   Chicago   San Diego

Visit *The Learning Site!*

www.harcourtschool.com

ISBN 0-15-326689-9

6 7 8 9 10   197   10 09 08 07 06 05 04 03

Ordering Options
ISBN 0-15-323767-8 (Collection)
ISBN 0-15-326723-2 (package of 5)

Contents

Muff's Bath

by J.C. Cunningham
illustrations by Mike Gordon

Muff is Bud's new pup.
Muff runs and jumps.

Muff runs and jumps
in the mud! Muff must
get a bath.

Bud fills a tub
with suds.
"Jump in, Muff!"

4

Bud tugs at Muff.
Huff! Puff!
Muff will not get
in the tub.

Bud hugs Muff.
"Baths are fun, Muff.
You'll see."

Bud rubs suds on Muff.
"Ruff! Ruff!"
Muff likes it!

Muff gets a bath, but
Bud gets a bath, too!

8

Buck Duck

by Gail Williams
illustrated by Marc Mongeau

Buck Duck packed
up his truck.

"I am a glad, glad
duck. Off I go in
my big, red truck!"

11

"I am NOT a glad,
glad duck! Look
at this mud.
I am stuck!"

A pup jumped up.
"I can help. Just
come with me."

The pup led Buck
up a path. The
pup's mom had
a big, pink bus.

Tug, tug. Huff, puff, puff. Bump, thump. Bump, thump. THUMP!

"I am a glad, glad
duck. Thanks a lot!
It's not fun if you
get stuck!"

Muff's Bath

Word Count: 74

High-Frequency Words

are
likes
new
see
the
too
you'll

Decodable Words*

a	**huff**	on
and	**hugs**	**puff**
at	in	**pup**
bath	is	**rubs**
baths	it	**ruff**
Bud	**jump**	**runs**
Bud's	**jumps**	**suds**
but	**mud**	**tub**
fills	**Muff**	**tugs**
fun	**Muff's**	will
get	**must**	with
gets	not	

*Words with /u/*u* appear in **boldface** type.

Buck Duck

Word Count: 88

High-Frequency Words

go
my
look
come
me
the
you

Decodable Words*

a	glad	led	**pup's**
am	had	lot	red
at	help	mom	**stuck**
big	his	**mud**	thanks
Buck	**huff**	not	this
bump	I	off	**thump**
bus	if	packed	**truck**
can	in	path	**tug**
Duck	it's	pink	**up**
fun	**jumped**	**puff**	with
get	**just**	**pup**	

*Words with /u/*u* appear in **boldface** type.